# Leading the Future: Transformative Strategies for Modern Leadership

Mastering the Art of Visionary Leadership in a Rapidly Changing World

BY: YOUSIF BSHIR

# Introduction

**Shaping Tomorrow: The Imperative of Leading the Future**

In a world where technological advancements and global shifts are occurring at an unprecedented pace, the role of leadership is undergoing a profound transformation. Modern leadership is no longer just about managing the present but about actively shaping the future. To lead effectively, you need more than traditional skills; you need a visionary mindset that anticipates trends, embraces innovation, and navigates through uncertainty with confidence.

This book is crafted to provide you with the insights and strategies necessary to excel in this dynamic environment. You'll learn how to develop a compelling vision that inspires and guides your team, leverage innovative practices to stay ahead of the curve, and build a resilient organization capable of turning challenges into opportunities.

**Purpose of This Book**

As you delve into these pages, you will discover:

- How to Cultivate a Visionary Mindset: Understand how to create and communicate a powerful vision that directs and motivates your team toward achieving future goals.
- How to Leverage Innovation: Explore practical ways to integrate new technologies and innovative approaches that keep you at the forefront of your industry.
- How to Build and Lead Resilient Teams: Learn strategies for forming and guiding teams that adapt and thrive amidst change.
- How to Transform Challenges into Opportunities: Gain techniques for managing crises and using them as springboards for growth and success.

By engaging with the concepts and strategies presented in this book, you'll be equipped to lead with purpose and foresight, positioning yourself and your organization for enduring success in an ever-evolving world.

# Chapter 1: Laying the Foundation for a Visionary Future

**Crafting a Strategic Vision**

Developing a strategic vision is a pivotal step in leading effectively and influencing the future. This vision not only defines where you want your organization to go but also motivates and aligns everyone toward common goals. Here's a detailed approach to crafting a vision that stands out:

1. **Clarify Core Values and Mission:**

    • Define Core Values: Identify the fundamental principles that guide your organization. These values should reflect your organization's identity and culture, shaping every aspect of its operations.

    • Articulate the Mission: Develop a clear mission statement that communicates your organization's purpose and goals. This mission serves as the foundation upon which your vision is built.

2. **Envision the Future:**

    • Set Ambitious Goals: Imagine where you want your organization to be in 5, 10, or 20 years. Consider factors like market position, technological advancements, and social impact.

    • Create a Vision Statement: Draft a vision statement that encapsulates your long-term objectives in a concise and inspiring manner. Ensure it is specific enough to provide direction yet broad enough to allow for flexibility.

3. **Engage Stakeholders:**

    • Involve Key Players: Engage with employees, customers, partners, and other stakeholders to gather diverse perspectives. This involvement can provide valuable insights and foster a sense of ownership.

    • Facilitate Workshops: Organize workshops or focus groups to collaboratively develop and refine the vision. This participatory approach helps in aligning the vision with the aspirations and expectations of those involved.

### 4. Communicate and Implement:

• Craft a Communication Plan: Develop a strategy for communicating your vision throughout the organization. Use multiple channels, including meetings, written communications, and digital platforms.

• Embed the Vision in Culture: Integrate the vision into the organizational culture by aligning policies, practices, and incentives with the vision. Ensure that it influences decision-making and behavior at all levels.

**Anticipating Future Changes**

Adapting to and anticipating future changes is essential for maintaining a competitive edge. This involves understanding global trends and innovations that could impact your organization's strategy. Here's how to effectively anticipate and prepare for future changes:

### 1. Conduct Comprehensive Trend Analysis:

• Identify Key Trends: Regularly review industry reports, market analyses, and emerging technologies. Pay attention to macro trends such as economic shifts, demographic changes, and regulatory developments.

• Analyze Implications: Assess how these trends could affect your industry and organization. Consider both opportunities and threats, and evaluate their potential impact on your strategic vision.

### 2. Engage in Scenario Planning:

• Develop Scenarios: Create multiple scenarios based on different future conditions. These scenarios should include best-case, worst-case, and most likely scenarios to prepare for various possibilities.

• Evaluate Responses: Determine how your organization would respond to each scenario. Develop contingency plans and strategies to mitigate risks and capitalize on opportunities.

### 3. Monitor and Benchmark Competitors:

• Track Competitor Movements: Regularly analyze the strategies and innovations of competitors. Identify trends in their approaches and anticipate their future moves.

• Benchmark Best Practices: Use competitor analysis to benchmark your organization's practices against industry leaders. This can help you identify gaps and areas for improvement.

**4. Foster a Culture of Innovation:**

•   Encourage Forward Thinking: Promote a culture where innovation and forward thinking are valued. Encourage team members to stay informed about emerging trends and to think creatively about potential changes.

•   Invest in Research and Development: Allocate resources to R&D to explore new technologies and solutions. This proactive approach can help you stay ahead of industry changes and integrate new innovations into your strategy.

By establishing a clear and compelling vision and staying vigilant about future changes, you can lead your organization with confidence, effectively navigate uncertainties, and position yourself as a forward-thinking leader in an ever-evolving world.

# Chapter 2: Developing an Innovative Mindset

**The Importance of Innovation**

Innovation is more than just a buzzword; it is a critical driver of leadership and organizational success. Embracing innovation can profoundly impact how you lead and how your organization thrives in a competitive landscape. Here's why innovation is crucial:

**1.   Driving Competitive Advantage:**

•   Differentiation: Innovative practices and products set your organization apart from competitors. They provide unique value propositions that attract customers and differentiate your brand.

•   Market Leadership: By leading with innovative solutions, you position your organization as a leader in your industry, setting trends rather than following them.

**2.   Enhancing Organizational Agility:**

•   Adaptability: Innovation fosters adaptability, enabling your organization to respond quickly to changing market conditions and emerging opportunities.

•   Resilience: An innovative mindset helps build resilience by encouraging creative problem-solving and flexibility in the face of challenges.

### 3. Boosting Employee Engagement:

• Motivation: Employees who are encouraged to innovate are more likely to be engaged and motivated. They feel valued and invested in the organization's success.

• Talent Attraction: A culture of innovation attracts top talent who are eager to contribute to forward-thinking and dynamic environments.

### 4. Driving Growth and Efficiency:

• New Revenue Streams: Innovation can lead to the development of new products, services, and business models, creating additional revenue streams.

• Operational Efficiency: Innovative processes and technologies can enhance operational efficiency, reducing costs and improving productivity.

## Fostering a Culture of Innovation

Creating an environment that supports and nurtures innovation requires deliberate strategies and practices. Here's how to build a culture that encourages new ideas and creativity:

### 1. Encourage Open Communication:

• Promote Idea Sharing: Foster an environment where team members feel comfortable sharing their ideas without fear of criticism. Open forums, brainstorming sessions, and idea management platforms can facilitate this.

• Provide Constructive Feedback: Offer feedback that is constructive and supportive. Encourage continuous dialogue about ideas and their potential impact.

### 2. Support Experimentation and Risk-Taking:

• Create Safe Spaces for Experimentation: Allow employees to test new ideas and approaches without the fear of failure. This can be done through pilot projects or innovation labs.

• Encourage Calculated Risks: Promote a mindset where taking informed risks is valued. Support initiatives that have potential but may involve uncertainty.

3. **Invest in Learning and Development:**

• Training and Workshops: Provide training programs and workshops focused on creativity, problem-solving, and innovative thinking. This helps build skills necessary for generating and implementing new ideas.

• Knowledge Sharing: Encourage continuous learning by sharing insights, case studies, and best practices from other organizations and industries.

4. **Recognize and Reward Innovation:**

• Celebrate Successes: Acknowledge and celebrate successful innovations and the individuals behind them. Recognition can be in the form of awards, public praise, or career advancement opportunities.

• Incentivize Contributions: Implement incentive programs that reward innovative contributions. This can include financial rewards, bonuses, or additional responsibilities.

5. **Lead by Example:**

• Model Innovative Behavior: As a leader, demonstrate innovative thinking and problem-solving in your own work. Show that you value and engage in creative processes.

• Champion Innovation Initiatives: Actively support and participate in innovation initiatives within the organization. Your involvement sets a positive example and encourages others to follow suit.

6. **Create Cross-Functional Teams:**

• Diverse Perspectives: Form cross-functional teams that bring together individuals from different departments and backgrounds. Diverse perspectives can lead to more creative solutions and innovative ideas.

• Collaborative Projects: Encourage collaboration on projects that require input from various areas of expertise. This approach can spark new ideas and enhance problem-solving.


By cultivating an innovative mindset and fostering a culture that supports creativity, you position your organization to continuously evolve and thrive in a rapidly changing world. Embracing innovation not only enhances leadership effectiveness but also drives long-term success and growth.

# Chapter 3: Leadership in the Age of Digital Transformation

## Adapting to Digital Transformation

Digital transformation is reshaping the way organizations operate, and effective leadership is crucial for navigating this change. Integrating technology into leadership strategies involves more than just adopting new tools; it requires a comprehensive approach to leveraging digital advancements for strategic success. Here's how to effectively incorporate technology into your leadership strategy:

1. **Develop a Digital Vision:**

• Define Digital Goals: Establish clear objectives for digital transformation that align with your organization's overall strategy. This includes identifying key areas where technology can drive growth, efficiency, and innovation.

• Create a Roadmap: Develop a detailed roadmap outlining the steps and milestones for integrating digital technologies. This should include timelines, resource allocation, and key performance indicators.

2. **Invest in Technology:**

• Evaluate Technological Needs: Assess the technology requirements of your organization. This involves identifying tools and platforms that can enhance operations, customer experience, and data management.

• Prioritize Upgrades: Focus on upgrading or acquiring technologies that offer the greatest potential for impact. Consider factors such as scalability, integration capabilities, and return on investment.

3. **Foster a Digital Culture:**

• Promote Digital Literacy: Ensure that all employees are equipped with the necessary skills and knowledge to effectively use digital tools. Offer training programs and resources to build digital competencies across the organization.

• Encourage Digital Collaboration: Implement platforms and tools that facilitate digital collaboration and communication. This can enhance teamwork and streamline workflows, especially in remote or hybrid work environments.

### 4. Leverage Data Analytics:

• Utilize Data for Decision-Making: Incorporate data analytics into your decision-making processes. Use data to gain insights into customer behavior, operational performance, and market trends.

• Enhance Predictive Capabilities: Employ predictive analytics to anticipate future trends and make proactive decisions. This can help in identifying opportunities and mitigating risks.

**Overcoming Digital Challenges**

Navigating the complexities of digital transformation presents various challenges. Here are strategies for managing these challenges effectively:

### 1. Address Resistance to Change:

• Communicate Clearly: Transparently communicate the benefits and objectives of digital transformation to all stakeholders. Address concerns and provide a clear rationale for the changes.

• Involve Key Stakeholders: Engage employees and other stakeholders early in the transformation process. Involvement in decision-making and implementation can reduce resistance and build support.

### 2. Manage Technological Integration:

• Ensure Seamless Integration: Plan and execute the integration of new technologies with existing systems carefully. Avoid disruptions by testing integrations and ensuring compatibility.

• Monitor Performance: Continuously monitor the performance of new technologies and make adjustments as needed. Regular reviews can help in identifying issues and optimizing performance.

### 3. Secure Digital Assets:

• Implement Robust Security Measures: Protect your organization's digital assets with strong cybersecurity protocols. This includes using encryption, multi-factor authentication, and regular security audits.

• Educate on Cybersecurity: Provide training to employees on best practices for cybersecurity. Awareness and vigilance are key to preventing data breaches and protecting sensitive information.

4. **Maintain Flexibility and Agility:**

• Adapt to Technological Advances: Stay informed about emerging technologies and trends. Be prepared to adapt your strategies and technologies as new advancements become available.

• Encourage Continuous Improvement: Foster a culture of continuous improvement and innovation. Encourage experimentation and iterative development to refine digital processes and solutions.

5. **Measure and Assess Impact:**

• Track Key Metrics: Establish metrics to measure the impact of digital transformation on organizational performance. This includes evaluating improvements in efficiency, customer satisfaction, and financial outcomes.

• Review and Adjust: Regularly review the results of digital initiatives and make necessary adjustments. Use feedback and performance data to refine strategies and enhance outcomes.

By effectively integrating technology into your leadership approach and addressing the challenges of digital transformation, you can drive your organization toward success in the digital age. Embracing these strategies ensures that you are well-equipped to leverage technology for strategic advantage, resilience, and growth.

## Chapter 4: Strategic Planning for Change

**Developing a Strategic Change Plan**

Effective strategic planning is crucial for managing change within an organization. A well-crafted change plan provides a structured approach to navigating transitions and achieving desired outcomes. Here's how to develop a comprehensive strategic change plan:

1. **Define the Scope of Change:**

• Identify Objectives: Clearly articulate the objectives of the change initiative. Determine what you aim to achieve, whether it's improving processes, adopting new technologies, or entering new markets.

• Assess Impact: Evaluate how the change will impact different areas of the organization. Consider effects on operations, employees, customers, and other stakeholders.

2. **Develop a Detailed Change Strategy:**

• Outline Key Steps: Create a step-by-step plan outlining the major phases of the change process. Include milestones, timelines, and key deliverables for each phase.

• Set Goals and Metrics: Establish specific, measurable goals and performance metrics to track progress. These should align with the overall objectives of the change initiative.

3. **Engage Stakeholders:**

• Communicate Vision: Clearly communicate the vision and rationale behind the change to all stakeholders. Use various channels to ensure that everyone is informed and aligned with the goals.

• Seek Input and Feedback: Involve stakeholders in the planning process to gather their insights and address any concerns. This helps in gaining buy-in and reducing resistance.

4. **Develop a Change Management Team:**

• Assign Roles and Responsibilities: Form a dedicated team responsible for overseeing the change process. Assign specific roles and responsibilities to team members based on their expertise and experience.

• Provide Training and Support: Equip the change management team with the necessary training and resources. Ensure they have the skills to lead and support the change effectively.

5. **Create a Communication Plan:**

• Design Communication Strategies: Develop a communication plan detailing how updates and information will be shared throughout the change process. Include methods for both formal and informal communication.

• Address Concerns: Provide channels for employees and stakeholders to raise questions and concerns. Address these proactively to maintain trust and transparency.

**Managing Resources Effectively**

Effective resource management is essential for the successful implementation of change. Proper allocation of resources and budgeting ensures that the change process is well-supported and that objectives are met. Here's how to manage resources effectively:

1. **Allocate Resources Strategically:**

• Identify Resource Needs: Determine the resources required for each phase of the change process, including personnel, technology, and financial resources.

• Prioritize Allocation: Allocate resources based on priority and impact. Focus on areas that will have the greatest effect on achieving change objectives.

2. **Develop a Budget:**

• Create a Detailed Budget: Prepare a comprehensive budget that outlines all costs associated with the change initiative. Include expenses for personnel, technology, training, and other resources.

• Monitor and Adjust: Regularly review budget performance and make adjustments as needed. Ensure that expenditures align with the planned budget and address any variances.

3. **Manage Financial Resources:**

• Track Expenditures: Implement systems to track and manage financial expenditures related to the change initiative. Ensure that spending stays within budgetary limits.

• Allocate Contingency Funds: Set aside contingency funds to address unforeseen costs or challenges that may arise during the change process.

4. **Optimize Human Resources:**

• Assign Roles Effectively: Match employees' skills and expertise with roles that are critical to the change process. Ensure that key positions are filled with individuals who can drive the change effectively.

• Provide Training and Support: Offer training and development programs to prepare employees for new roles or responsibilities. Support them in adapting to new processes and technologies.

5. **Leverage Technology and Tools:**

• Implement Supportive Tools: Use technology and tools that facilitate the change process. This may include project management software, communication platforms, and performance tracking systems.

• Ensure Integration: Ensure that new technologies are integrated smoothly with existing systems and processes. Provide training to employees on how to use these tools effectively.

By developing a comprehensive strategic change plan and managing resources effectively, you can navigate the complexities of organizational change with confidence. A well-structured approach ensures that the change process is smooth, resources are utilized efficiently, and desired outcomes are achieved.

## Chapter 5: Building a Strong and Sustainable Team

**Forming the Ideal Team**

Creating an effective team requires a strategic approach to selecting individuals and fostering collaboration. Here's how to build a team that is both strong and sustainable:

1. **Define Team Objectives and Roles:**

    • Establish Clear Objectives: Identify the goals and objectives the team needs to achieve. Ensure that each team member understands these objectives and how their role contributes to them.

    • Determine Roles and Responsibilities: Clearly define roles and responsibilities for each team member. Ensure that the distribution of tasks aligns with individual strengths and expertise.

2. **Select the Right Individuals:**

    • Assess Skills and Experience: Evaluate candidates based on their skills, experience, and fit with the team's needs. Use structured interviews, assessments, and reference checks to make informed decisions.

    • Consider Cultural Fit: Choose individuals who align with the organization's values and culture. A good cultural fit enhances team cohesion and overall effectiveness.

3. **Foster Team Dynamics:**

    • Promote Collaboration: Create opportunities for team members to work together on projects and initiatives. Encourage open communication and collaborative problem-solving.

    • Build Trust: Foster trust among team members through transparency, reliability, and support. Trust is essential for effective teamwork and achieving shared goals.

4. **Provide Training and Development:**

• Offer Onboarding Programs: Implement comprehensive onboarding programs to help new team members integrate smoothly. Provide training on team processes, tools, and expectations.

• Support Continuous Learning: Encourage ongoing professional development and skill-building. Offer opportunities for team members to attend workshops, courses, and conferences.

5. **Monitor and Evaluate Team Performance:**

• Set Performance Metrics: Establish clear metrics to measure team performance. Regularly review progress and provide feedback to ensure that the team stays on track.

• Conduct Performance Reviews: Hold regular performance reviews to assess individual and team performance. Use these reviews to identify areas for improvement and celebrate successes.

**Managing Diverse Teams**

Managing teams with diverse backgrounds and experiences requires thoughtful strategies to harness their strengths and address potential challenges. Here's how to effectively manage diverse teams:

1. **Embrace and Leverage Diversity:**

• Value Different Perspectives: Recognize the value of diverse perspectives and experiences. Encourage team members to share their unique viewpoints and ideas.

• Promote Inclusivity: Create an inclusive environment where everyone feels valued and respected. Implement policies and practices that support diversity and inclusion.

2. **Facilitate Effective Communication:**

• Encourage Open Dialogue: Foster an environment where open dialogue is encouraged. Address communication barriers by providing language support or cultural sensitivity training.

• Use Multiple Channels: Utilize various communication channels to ensure that information is accessible to all team members. This may include written documents, meetings, and digital platforms.

### 3. Build Cultural Competence:

- Provide Cultural Training: Offer training programs that increase cultural awareness and sensitivity. Educate team members about different cultural norms and practices.

- Promote Understanding and Respect: Encourage team members to learn about and respect each other's cultural backgrounds. Facilitate activities that build cultural understanding and appreciation.

### 4. Manage Conflicts Constructively:

- Address Conflicts Early: Tackle conflicts and misunderstandings promptly to prevent escalation. Use conflict resolution techniques that focus on finding mutually acceptable solutions.

- Foster a Positive Environment: Create a supportive environment where conflicts can be addressed constructively. Encourage a culture of collaboration and problem-solving.

### 5. Encourage Team Building:

- Organize Team-Building Activities: Plan team-building activities that promote collaboration and strengthen relationships. These activities can help break down barriers and build trust.

- Celebrate Diversity: Recognize and celebrate the diverse backgrounds and contributions of team members. Highlight achievements and milestones that reflect the team's diversity.

By forming the right team and managing diversity effectively, you can build a strong, cohesive, and sustainable team that drives success and innovation. Embracing diverse perspectives and fostering a supportive environment will enhance team performance and contribute to long-term organizational growth.

# Chapter 6: Ethical Leadership and Social Responsibility

## The Importance of Ethical Leadership

Ethical leadership is crucial for building trust, credibility, and a positive reputation within an organization and its community. Here's how ethical leadership contributes to organizational success:

1. **Building Trust and Credibility:**

    • Consistency and Integrity: Ethical leaders demonstrate consistency between their words and actions, reinforcing their integrity. This reliability fosters trust among employees, stakeholders, and customers.

    • Transparency: Ethical leaders practice transparency in decision-making and communication. Being open about intentions and actions helps build confidence and reduces skepticism.

2. **Enhancing Organizational Reputation:**

    • Positive Image: Organizations led by ethical leaders are viewed positively by the public, which enhances their reputation and attractiveness to customers, investors, and partners.

    • Reputation Management: Ethical behavior helps in managing and protecting the organization's reputation. It minimizes the risk of scandals and negative publicity that could arise from unethical practices.

3. **Fostering a Positive Work Environment:**

    • Employee Morale: An ethical work environment promotes fairness and respect, boosting employee morale and job satisfaction. Employees are more likely to feel valued and motivated.

    • Ethical Culture: Ethical leadership sets the tone for an ethical organizational culture. Leaders who model ethical behavior encourage employees to adhere to similar standards.

4. **Driving Long-Term Success:**

    • Sustainable Practices: Ethical leadership supports sustainable business practices that contribute to long-term success. It aligns organizational goals with societal values and expectations.

    • Risk Mitigation: Ethical practices reduce the risk of legal issues and compliance violations. This proactive approach helps avoid potential pitfalls and legal challenges.

**Integrating Social Responsibility**

Incorporating social responsibility into your organization's strategy involves implementing initiatives that benefit society while aligning with organizational values and goals. Here's how to successfully execute social responsibility initiatives:

1. **Develop a Social Responsibility Strategy:**

    • Define Objectives: Identify the social and environmental issues that align with your organization's values and mission. Set clear objectives for your social responsibility initiatives.

    • Create a Plan: Develop a strategic plan that outlines the initiatives you will undertake, including specific goals, timelines, and resources required.

2. **Engage Stakeholders:**

    • Involve Key Stakeholders: Engage employees, customers, suppliers, and community members in your social responsibility efforts. Their input can help shape initiatives and ensure they address relevant issues.

    • Communicate Initiatives: Clearly communicate your social responsibility goals and activities to stakeholders. Transparency in your efforts builds support and demonstrates commitment.

3. **Implement Initiatives:**

    • Launch Programs: Initiate programs and projects that address social and environmental issues. This may include charitable contributions, environmental sustainability efforts, or community development activities.

    • Integrate with Core Operations: Align social responsibility initiatives with core business operations. Ensure that your efforts are integrated into the organization's overall strategy and daily activities.

4. **Measure and Evaluate Impact:**

    • Track Progress: Establish metrics to measure the impact of your social responsibility initiatives. Regularly assess progress toward goals and evaluate the effectiveness of your programs.

    • Report Results: Provide transparent reports on the outcomes of your initiatives. Share success stories, challenges, and lessons learned with stakeholders to maintain credibility and accountability.

**5. Foster Continuous Improvement:**

• Seek Feedback: Solicit feedback from stakeholders and employees on your social responsibility efforts. Use this feedback to make improvements and adapt your strategies.

• Innovate and Evolve: Continuously explore new ways to enhance your social responsibility initiatives. Stay informed about emerging trends and best practices to ensure your efforts remain relevant and impactful.

**6. Promote Ethical Practices Across the Organization:**

• Training and Awareness: Implement training programs to educate employees about ethical practices and social responsibility. Promote awareness and understanding of these principles throughout the organization.

• Encourage Participation: Foster a culture where employees are encouraged to participate in social responsibility activities and contribute ideas for new initiatives.

By prioritizing ethical leadership and integrating social responsibility into your organizational strategy, you can enhance trust, build a positive reputation, and contribute to societal well-being. These practices not only drive organizational success but also create a lasting positive impact on the community and environment.

## Chapter 7: Enhancing Communication Skills

**Effective Communication Strategies**

Effective communication is vital for successful leadership and organizational performance. Enhancing your communication skills can improve interactions with all stakeholders and ensure that your messages are clear and impactful. Here's how to develop and apply effective communication strategies:

**1. Develop Clear and Concise Messaging:**

• Articulate Objectives: Clearly define the purpose and objectives of your communication. Ensure that your message is focused and directly addresses the intended goals.

• Use Simple Language: Avoid jargon and complex language that may confuse your audience. Use simple, straightforward language to convey your message effectively.

### 2. Enhance Active Listening Skills:

- Practice Active Listening: Pay full attention to the speaker, show empathy, and provide feedback. Active listening helps you understand the speaker's perspective and respond appropriately.

- Ask Clarifying Questions: When needed, ask questions to clarify points and ensure a thorough understanding of the message being communicated.

### 3. Utilize Non-Verbal Communication:

- Be Mindful of Body Language: Pay attention to your body language, facial expressions, and gestures. Ensure that non-verbal cues align with your verbal message to reinforce clarity.

- Maintain Eye Contact: Establish and maintain eye contact to convey confidence and engagement. This helps build trust and demonstrates attentiveness.

### 4. Adapt Communication Style to the Audience:

- Assess Audience Needs: Tailor your communication style to fit the needs and preferences of your audience. Consider factors such as their level of knowledge, interests, and communication preferences.

- Use Appropriate Channels: Choose the most effective communication channels based on the audience and the message. This may include emails, meetings, presentations, or digital platforms.

### 5. Provide Constructive Feedback:

- Offer Specific Feedback: When giving feedback, be specific and provide actionable suggestions. Focus on behavior and performance rather than personal attributes.

- Encourage Open Dialogue: Create an environment where feedback is encouraged and welcomed. Foster open dialogue and constructive discussions to promote continuous improvement.

### 6. Enhance Presentation Skills:

- Prepare Thoroughly: Plan and prepare for presentations in advance. Organize your content logically, and use visual aids to support your message.

- Engage the Audience: Use engaging techniques such as storytelling, interactive elements, and questions to captivate your audience and maintain their interest.

**Managing Rumors and Misinformation**

Effectively handling rumors and misinformation is essential for maintaining credibility and trust. Here's how to manage and address inaccurate information:

1. **Monitor Information Flow:**

    • Stay Informed: Keep track of emerging rumors and misinformation related to your organization. Use monitoring tools and maintain awareness of social media and news sources.

    • Identify Sources: Determine the origin and credibility of the information. Assess whether it's coming from reliable sources or if it's based on unfounded claims.

2. **Address Misinformation Proactively:**

    • Provide Accurate Information: Counter misinformation by providing accurate and factual information. Use official statements, data, and evidence to refute false claims.

    • Communicate Transparently: Be transparent about the situation and your organization's stance. Clearly communicate the steps being taken to address the issue and provide updates as necessary.

3. **Engage with Stakeholders:**

    • Respond to Inquiries: Address questions and concerns from stakeholders promptly. Provide clear and accurate responses to mitigate confusion and maintain trust.

    • Correct False Information: If misinformation is spreading, correct it directly through official channels. Use press releases, social media, and other platforms to clarify the facts.

4. **Implement Crisis Communication Plans:**

    • Develop a Crisis Plan: Prepare a crisis communication plan that outlines procedures for managing misinformation and rumors. Include roles, responsibilities, and communication strategies.

    • Train Spokespersons: Ensure that designated spokespersons are trained in handling misinformation and delivering consistent messages. Provide them with the necessary resources and support.

5. **Build a Positive Reputation:**

    • Foster Trust: Build and maintain a positive reputation through consistent, transparent, and ethical communication. A strong reputation helps counteract the effects of misinformation.

- **Engage with the Community:** Develop strong relationships with the community and stakeholders. Active engagement and positive interactions can help build resilience against misinformation.

6. **Evaluate and Adapt:**

- **Review Communication Effectiveness:** Regularly assess the effectiveness of your communication strategies in managing misinformation. Identify areas for improvement and adapt your approach as needed.

- **Learn from Incidents:** Analyze past incidents of misinformation to understand what worked well and what could be improved. Use these insights to enhance your future communication strategies.

By mastering effective communication strategies and managing misinformation proactively, you can enhance your leadership effectiveness and maintain a positive organizational reputation. Clear, transparent, and empathetic communication fosters trust and credibility with all stakeholders.

## Chapter 8: Fostering and Supporting Innovation

**Inspiring Individuals to Innovate**

Encouraging creativity and innovation among team members is essential for driving progress and achieving competitive advantage. Here's how to motivate individuals and teams to generate new ideas:

1. **Create a Culture of Innovation:**

- **Promote Openness:** Foster an environment where employees feel comfortable sharing their ideas. Encourage open dialogue and show appreciation for all contributions.

- **Encourage Experimentation:** Allow team members to experiment with new ideas without fear of failure. Support risk-taking and learning from mistakes as part of the innovation process.

2. **Provide Resources and Support:**

• Allocate Time and Resources: Provide dedicated time and resources for employees to work on innovative projects. This could include innovation labs, brainstorming sessions, or access to new tools and technologies.

• Offer Training and Development: Invest in training programs that enhance creative thinking and problem-solving skills. Provide workshops, seminars, and other resources to help employees develop their innovative capabilities.

3. **Recognize and Reward Innovation:**

• Celebrate Successes: Acknowledge and celebrate successful innovations and contributions. Use recognition programs, awards, and public acknowledgments to motivate and inspire others.

• Provide Incentives: Offer incentives for innovative ideas and achievements. This could include bonuses, promotions, or opportunities for career advancement.

4. **Encourage Collaboration and Idea Sharing:**

• Facilitate Teamwork: Promote collaboration across teams and departments to generate diverse perspectives and ideas. Use collaborative tools and create opportunities for cross-functional interactions.

• Organize Innovation Challenges: Host innovation challenges or hackathons to stimulate creativity and problem-solving. Provide a platform for employees to present and develop their ideas.

5. **Lead by Example:**

• Model Innovative Behavior: Demonstrate a commitment to innovation through your own actions. Share your own ideas, engage in creative problem-solving, and support innovative initiatives.

• Encourage Curiosity: Show curiosity and a willingness to explore new possibilities. Engage with emerging trends and technologies to inspire your team.

## Evaluating and Implementing Ideas

Turning innovative ideas into practical and successful projects involves careful evaluation and strategic implementation. Here's how to assess and execute innovative ideas effectively:

1. **Establish Evaluation Criteria:**

    • Define Success Metrics: Develop clear criteria for evaluating ideas, including factors such as feasibility, impact, cost, and alignment with organizational goals.

    • Assess Potential: Evaluate the potential of each idea based on its originality, market demand, and alignment with strategic objectives.

2. **Conduct Feasibility Studies:**

    • Analyze Viability: Perform feasibility studies to assess the practicality of implementing the idea. This includes evaluating technical, financial, and operational aspects.

    • Identify Risks: Identify potential risks and challenges associated with the idea. Develop strategies to mitigate these risks and address any obstacles.

3. **Develop a Project Plan:**

    • Create a Detailed Plan: Develop a comprehensive project plan that outlines the steps for implementing the idea. Include timelines, resource requirements, and key milestones.

    • Assign Responsibilities: Assign roles and responsibilities for executing the project. Ensure that team members have the necessary skills and resources to contribute effectively.

4. **Pilot and Test:**

    • Conduct Pilot Programs: Implement pilot programs or prototypes to test the idea on a smaller scale. Gather feedback and make necessary adjustments before full-scale implementation.

    • Evaluate Results: Assess the results of the pilot program to determine the effectiveness of the idea. Use this feedback to refine the concept and improve its viability.

5. **Implement and Scale:**

    • Execute the Plan: Once the idea is refined, proceed with full-scale implementation. Monitor progress and ensure that the project stays on track with the established plan.

    • Scale Up: If the project proves successful, develop strategies for scaling up and expanding its impact. Consider additional markets, applications, or opportunities for growth.

**6. Monitor and Evaluate Performance:**

• Track Outcomes: Continuously monitor the performance of the implemented idea. Track key performance indicators and measure success against the defined criteria.

• Gather Feedback: Solicit feedback from stakeholders, including customers, employees, and partners. Use this input to make further improvements and adjustments.

**7. Document and Share Learnings:**

• Document Successes and Failures: Record the outcomes of the innovation process, including successes and challenges. Document lessons learned to inform future innovation efforts.

• Share Insights: Share insights and best practices with the organization. Foster a culture of learning and continuous improvement by disseminating knowledge gained from innovative projects.

By fostering a culture of innovation and implementing a structured approach to evaluating and executing ideas, you can drive meaningful progress and maintain a competitive edge. Supporting creativity and ensuring effective execution of innovative ideas are key to achieving long-term success and growth.

# Chapter 9: Managing Cultural Change

**Transforming Organizational Culture**

Successfully managing and transforming organizational culture is crucial for supporting and sustaining change. Here's how to effectively manage and develop organizational culture to align with change initiatives:

**1. Define the Desired Culture:**

• Articulate Cultural Goals: Clearly define the aspects of the culture you want to change or enhance. Identify the values, behaviors, and practices that align with your change objectives.

• Develop a Vision: Create a vision for the desired organizational culture. This vision should reflect the goals of the change initiative and provide a clear direction for cultural transformation.

**2. Engage Leadership and Stakeholders:**

• Secure Leadership Support: Gain commitment from senior leaders who can champion the cultural change. Their support is critical for modeling the desired behaviors and influencing others.

• Involve Key Stakeholders: Engage key stakeholders throughout the process. Involve employees, managers, and other relevant parties in discussions about the cultural changes and how they will be implemented.

**3. Communicate the Change:**

• Articulate the Need for Change: Clearly communicate the reasons for the cultural change and its benefits. Use various communication channels to reach different audiences within the organization.

• Share Success Stories: Highlight examples of successful cultural changes and the positive outcomes achieved. Use these stories to reinforce the value of the new culture and inspire others.

**4. Align Systems and Processes:**

• Adjust Policies and Procedures: Review and revise organizational policies, procedures, and practices to support the desired culture. Ensure that these elements reinforce the new cultural norms.

• Integrate Culture into Performance Management: Incorporate cultural values into performance management and evaluation processes. Recognize and reward behaviors that align with the desired culture.

**5. Provide Training and Development:**

• Offer Cultural Training: Provide training programs that educate employees about the new cultural values and expectations. Focus on developing skills and behaviors that support the change.

• Facilitate Workshops and Seminars: Conduct workshops and seminars to foster understanding and engagement with the new culture. Use these sessions to address concerns and build buy-in.

### 6. Support and Reinforce Change:

• Provide Ongoing Support: Offer support and resources to help employees adapt to the new culture. Provide coaching, mentorship, and assistance as needed.

• Reinforce Cultural Change: Continuously reinforce the new cultural values through regular communication, recognition, and celebrations. Ensure that the new culture becomes ingrained in daily practices.

## Measuring the Impact of Cultural Change

Assessing the impact of cultural changes is essential for understanding their effectiveness and making necessary adjustments. Here's how to evaluate the impact of cultural transformation on organizational performance:

### 1. Establish Key Performance Indicators (KPIs):

• Define Metrics: Identify specific metrics and indicators that reflect the success of the cultural change. These could include employee engagement, productivity, and retention rates.

• Set Baselines: Establish baseline measurements for the KPIs before implementing cultural changes. This allows for comparison and assessment of progress over time.

### 2. Conduct Surveys and Assessments:

• Administer Surveys: Use employee surveys to gather feedback on the cultural change. Assess perceptions, attitudes, and satisfaction related to the new culture.

• Perform Culture Audits: Conduct culture audits to evaluate the alignment between organizational practices and the desired culture. Identify gaps and areas for improvement.

### 3. Analyze Performance Data:

• Review Performance Metrics: Analyze data related to organizational performance, such as financial results, customer satisfaction, and operational efficiency. Assess whether improvements are linked to cultural changes.

• Track Employee Metrics: Monitor metrics related to employee performance, engagement, and turnover. Evaluate whether changes in these areas correlate with the new cultural norms.

**4. Gather Qualitative Feedback:**

• Conduct Interviews and Focus Groups: Hold interviews and focus groups with employees and leaders to gather qualitative insights. Understand how the cultural change has affected their work experiences and interactions.

• Solicit Feedback from Stakeholders: Engage with external stakeholders, such as customers and partners, to gather their perspectives on the cultural changes and their impact.

**5. Monitor Organizational Behavior:**

• Observe Behavioral Changes: Observe changes in organizational behavior and practices. Assess whether employees are adopting the new cultural values and norms in their daily activities.

• Evaluate Leadership Actions: Review how leaders are embodying and promoting the new culture. Ensure that their actions align with the desired cultural changes.

**6. Make Data-Driven Adjustments:**

• Identify Areas for Improvement: Based on the data and feedback, identify areas where the cultural change may need adjustment. Develop and implement strategies to address any challenges or gaps.

• Adapt Strategies: Continuously refine and adapt your approach to cultural change based on ongoing evaluation and feedback. Ensure that the cultural transformation remains relevant and effective.

**7. Communicate Results and Progress:**

• Share Impact Findings: Communicate the results of the cultural change assessment to employees and stakeholders. Highlight successes, challenges, and ongoing efforts to reinforce the new culture.

• Celebrate Achievements: Recognize and celebrate milestones and achievements related to the cultural change. Use these opportunities to reinforce commitment to the new culture.

By effectively managing cultural change and measuring its impact, you can ensure that the transformation is successful and sustainable. A well-managed cultural change enhances organizational performance, aligns with strategic goals, and supports long-term success.

# Chapter 10: Leading Through Crises

## Crisis Management Strategies

Effectively managing crises is essential for minimizing damage and guiding an organization through challenging situations. Here's how to handle crises with confidence and effectiveness:

1. **Develop a Crisis Management Plan:**

   • Create a Comprehensive Plan: Develop a detailed crisis management plan outlining procedures for various types of crises. Include protocols for response, communication, and recovery.

   • Establish Roles and Responsibilities: Define roles and responsibilities for the crisis management team. Ensure that team members understand their duties and have the necessary resources to act.

2. **Assess and Prioritize Risks:**

   • Identify Potential Risks: Conduct a risk assessment to identify potential crises that could impact the organization. Evaluate the likelihood and potential impact of each risk.

   • Prioritize Risks: Prioritize risks based on their potential severity and likelihood. Focus on addressing high-priority risks with well-defined response strategies.

3. **Implement Response Strategies:**

   • Activate the Crisis Management Team: Mobilize the crisis management team and execute the response plan. Ensure that all team members are informed and ready to take action.

   • Execute Contingency Plans: Implement contingency plans to address the immediate needs of the organization. Take swift and decisive actions to mitigate the impact of the crisis.

4. **Monitor and Adapt:**

   • Monitor the Situation: Continuously monitor the crisis situation and gather relevant information. Assess the effectiveness of the response and make adjustments as needed.

   • Adapt Strategies: Be flexible and adapt response strategies based on new information and changing circumstances. Ensure that the organization remains agile and responsive.

### 5. Coordinate with External Agencies:

- **Engage with Authorities:** Coordinate with external agencies, such as emergency services and regulatory bodies. Ensure that communication and collaboration are effective and aligned with the overall response strategy.

- **Seek Expert Advice:** Consult with experts and advisors to gain insights and support. Utilize their expertise to enhance your crisis management efforts.

### 6. Focus on Recovery and Resilience:

- **Develop a Recovery Plan:** Create a recovery plan to guide the organization through the post-crisis phase. Outline steps for restoring normal operations and addressing any residual impacts.

- **Build Resilience:** Use lessons learned from the crisis to strengthen organizational resilience. Implement improvements and preventive measures to better prepare for future challenges.

## Communication During Crises

Effective communication is critical for managing crises and maintaining trust with stakeholders. Here's how to ensure effective communication throughout a crisis:

### 1. Establish Clear Communication Channels:

- **Identify Key Channels:** Determine the most effective communication channels for reaching different stakeholders. This may include emails, press releases, social media, or internal messaging systems.

- **Ensure Accessibility:** Make sure that communication channels are accessible to all relevant parties. Provide updates through multiple channels to ensure comprehensive reach.

### 2. Communicate Transparently and Honestly:

- **Provide Accurate Information:** Share accurate and timely information about the crisis and response efforts. Avoid speculation and provide factual updates to build trust and credibility.

- **Acknowledge Uncertainties:** Be honest about uncertainties and unknowns. Address any gaps in information and provide assurances about efforts to resolve the situation.

3. **Maintain Consistent Messaging:**

• Develop Key Messages: Create clear and consistent key messages to convey to stakeholders. Ensure that all communications align with these messages to avoid confusion and mixed signals.

• Coordinate Messaging Across Teams: Ensure that all team members involved in communication are aligned with the key messages. Avoid conflicting information by coordinating messaging efforts.

4. **Engage and Support Employees:**

• Provide Regular Updates: Keep employees informed with regular updates about the crisis and its impact on the organization. Address their concerns and provide guidance on any changes or actions required.

• Offer Support: Provide support to employees affected by the crisis. This may include access to counseling services, temporary changes in work arrangements, or other forms of assistance.

5. **Manage External Communications:**

• Engage with Media: Communicate with media outlets to provide accurate information and manage public perception. Designate a spokesperson to handle media inquiries and ensure that messages are consistent.

• Respond to Inquiries: Address inquiries from external stakeholders, such as customers, partners, and regulators. Provide clear and timely responses to maintain trust and credibility.

6. **Monitor and Evaluate Communication Effectiveness:**

• Track Feedback: Monitor feedback from stakeholders and assess the effectiveness of your communication efforts. Use feedback to make adjustments and improve communication strategies.

• Analyze Communication Impact: Evaluate the impact of your communication on stakeholder perceptions and crisis management outcomes. Identify areas for improvement and incorporate lessons learned into future communication plans.

### 7. Document and Review:

• Document Communication Efforts: Keep detailed records of communication activities, decisions, and responses during the crisis. This documentation will be valuable for post-crisis analysis and future reference.

• Conduct a Post-Crisis Review: After the crisis, conduct a review of your communication efforts and overall crisis management. Analyze successes and areas for improvement to enhance future crisis response capabilities.

By implementing effective crisis management strategies and maintaining clear, transparent communication, you can navigate crises more effectively and support your organization through challenging situations. Effective leadership during crises not only addresses immediate concerns but also helps in building long-term resilience and trust.

## Chapter 11: Measuring and Evaluating Performance

### Defining Performance Indicators

To effectively measure the success of leadership strategies and innovations, it's essential to establish clear performance indicators. Here's how to define and implement these indicators:

### 1. Identify Key Objectives:

• Align with Goals: Ensure that the performance indicators are aligned with the organizational goals and objectives. Define what success looks like for each initiative or strategy.

• Specify Desired Outcomes: Clearly outline the outcomes you aim to achieve. This helps in identifying the most relevant indicators for measuring success.

### 2. Develop Relevant Metrics:

• Select Quantitative Metrics: Choose quantitative metrics that provide measurable data, such as revenue growth, market share, or cost reductions. These metrics offer concrete evidence of performance.

• Include Qualitative Metrics: Incorporate qualitative metrics that assess aspects such as employee satisfaction, customer feedback, and innovation impact. These metrics provide insights into the quality of performance.

**3. Establish Benchmark Standards:**

• Define Benchmarks: Set benchmarks or target standards for each performance indicator. These benchmarks can be based on historical data, industry standards, or competitive performance.

• Measure Progress: Regularly compare performance against these benchmarks to assess progress and determine whether targets are being met.

**4. Use Balanced Scorecards:**

• Implement a Balanced Scorecard: Use a balanced scorecard approach to track performance across multiple perspectives, including financial, customer, internal processes, and learning and growth.

• Integrate Metrics: Integrate financial and non-financial metrics to provide a comprehensive view of performance. This approach ensures that all aspects of success are considered.

**5. Involve Stakeholders:**

• Engage Stakeholders: Involve key stakeholders in defining performance indicators. Their input ensures that the metrics are relevant and reflect their expectations and concerns.

• Gather Feedback: Collect feedback from stakeholders on the effectiveness of the performance indicators. Use this feedback to refine and adjust the metrics as needed.

**Analyzing Results**

Evaluating the results of leadership strategies and innovations involves analyzing performance data to assess effectiveness and identify areas for improvement. Here's how to conduct a thorough analysis:

**1. Collect and Review Data:**

• Gather Performance Data: Collect data related to the defined performance indicators. This data can come from various sources, such as financial reports, surveys, and operational metrics.

• Review Trends and Patterns: Analyze the data to identify trends and patterns. Look for changes over time, correlations between metrics, and areas of concern.

## 2. Assess Achievement of Objectives:

- Evaluate Goal Attainment: Determine whether the objectives and targets have been achieved. Compare actual performance against the established benchmarks and goals.

- Analyze Success Factors: Identify the factors that contributed to achieving or failing to meet the objectives. Assess the impact of different strategies and initiatives.

## 3. Identify Strengths and Weaknesses:

- Highlight Strengths: Recognize areas where performance exceeded expectations. Analyze what contributed to these successes and how these strengths can be leveraged in future initiatives.

- Address Weaknesses: Identify areas where performance fell short of targets. Investigate the underlying causes and develop strategies to address these weaknesses.

## 4. Conduct Root Cause Analysis:

- Analyze Underlying Issues: Use root cause analysis techniques to understand the underlying issues affecting performance. This approach helps in identifying the root causes of problems rather than just addressing symptoms.

- Develop Action Plans: Create action plans to address identified issues. Focus on implementing changes that will improve performance and prevent recurrence of problems.

## 5. Implement Continuous Improvement:

- Promote a Culture of Improvement: Foster a culture of continuous improvement within the organization. Encourage regular review and refinement of strategies based on performance data.

- Apply Lessons Learned: Use insights gained from performance analysis to inform future strategies. Apply lessons learned to enhance effectiveness and drive innovation.

## 6. Communicate Results and Actions:

- Share Findings: Communicate the results of the performance analysis to relevant stakeholders. Provide a clear and transparent overview of what was achieved and what needs improvement.

- Outline Improvement Actions: Clearly outline the actions being taken to address performance issues. Ensure that stakeholders understand the steps being implemented and their expected impact.

### 7. Monitor Progress and Adjust:

• Track Implementation: Monitor the progress of improvement initiatives and ensure that changes are being effectively implemented. Track the impact of these changes on performance.

• Adjust Strategies: Be prepared to adjust strategies based on ongoing analysis and feedback. Continuously refine approaches to enhance performance and achieve desired outcomes.

By defining clear performance indicators and conducting thorough analyses of results, you can effectively measure the success of leadership strategies and innovations. This approach ensures that performance is continuously evaluated and improved, leading to sustained organizational success and growth.

## Chapter 12: Innovation Across Generations

**Managing Generational Diversity**

Effectively managing generational diversity within the workplace can enhance innovation by leveraging the unique perspectives and skills of different age groups. Here's how to harness generational diversity to drive innovation:

### 1. Recognize Generational Strengths:

• Identify Unique Contributions: Understand the strengths and contributions of each generation. For example, Baby Boomers may offer experience and stability, while Millennials and Gen Z may bring digital fluency and fresh perspectives.

• Leverage Diverse Skills: Use the varied skills and viewpoints of different generations to foster innovation. Encourage collaboration and cross-generational projects to integrate diverse ideas.

### 2. Create Inclusive Environments:

• Foster a Culture of Inclusion: Promote an inclusive culture that values the contributions of all generations. Ensure that all employees feel respected and valued for their unique perspectives.

• Encourage Knowledge Sharing: Facilitate knowledge sharing between generations. Use mentorship programs, workshops, and collaborative projects to bridge knowledge gaps and enhance learning.

3. **Utilize Diverse Teams:**

• Form Cross-Generational Teams: Build teams with members from different generations to promote diverse thinking and problem-solving. This diversity can lead to more innovative solutions and approaches.

• Balance Perspectives: Ensure that teams have a balanced representation of different age groups. This balance helps in capturing a wide range of ideas and experiences.

4. **Provide Tailored Resources:**

• Offer Diverse Training Programs: Design training programs that address the needs and preferences of different generations. This could include digital skills training for older employees and leadership development for younger employees.

• Customize Communication Channels: Use a variety of communication channels to reach different generations effectively. Adapt messaging and methods to suit the preferences of each group.

5. **Encourage Intergenerational Collaboration:**

• Promote Collaborative Projects: Create opportunities for intergenerational collaboration on projects and initiatives. Encourage team members to work together and share their insights and expertise.

• Host Innovation Workshops: Organize workshops and brainstorming sessions that include participants from different generations. Facilitate discussions and activities that encourage the exchange of ideas.

**Managing and Motivating Diverse Teams**

Effective management and motivation of teams across different age groups require understanding their unique needs and preferences. Here's how to manage and inspire a multigenerational workforce:

1. **Understand Motivational Drivers:**

• Identify What Drives Each Generation: Understand the motivational drivers for each generation, such as career development, work-life balance, and recognition. Tailor your management approach to address these needs.

• Offer Flexibility: Provide flexible work arrangements and benefits that appeal to different generations. This could include remote work options, flexible hours, or professional development opportunities.

**2. Provide Opportunities for Growth:**

• Support Career Development: Offer career development programs that cater to different career stages and aspirations. Provide opportunities for skill-building, leadership development, and career advancement.

• Encourage Continuous Learning: Promote a culture of continuous learning and growth. Provide access to training, workshops, and educational resources to help employees develop new skills and knowledge.

**3. Implement Effective Communication Strategies:**

• Adapt Communication Styles: Use communication styles that resonate with different generations. For example, Millennials and Gen Z may prefer digital communication, while older generations may favor face-to-face interactions.

• Encourage Open Dialogue: Foster an environment of open communication where employees feel comfortable sharing their ideas and feedback. Actively listen to their concerns and suggestions.

**4. Recognize and Reward Contributions:**

• Tailor Recognition Programs: Design recognition programs that acknowledge the contributions of employees from different generations. Use a variety of recognition methods, such as public praise, awards, and career advancement opportunities.

• Celebrate Achievements: Celebrate the achievements and milestones of team members from all generations. Recognize individual and team successes in ways that resonate with each generation.

**5. Build Strong Relationships:**

• Foster Team Building: Organize team-building activities that bring together employees from different generations. These activities can help build relationships, enhance collaboration, and improve team dynamics.

• Encourage Mentorship: Implement mentorship programs where employees from different generations can learn from each other. This can help bridge generational gaps and facilitate knowledge transfer.

6. **Address and Resolve Conflicts:**

• Manage Conflicts Constructively: Address conflicts between generations promptly and constructively. Use conflict resolution techniques to find common ground and foster mutual understanding.

• Promote Respectful Interactions: Encourage respectful interactions and collaboration among team members. Set clear expectations for behavior and communication to maintain a positive work environment.

7. **Evaluate and Adjust Strategies:**

• Monitor Team Dynamics: Regularly assess team dynamics and performance to ensure that strategies for managing and motivating diverse teams are effective. Use surveys, feedback, and performance metrics to evaluate success.

• Adapt Management Approaches: Be prepared to adjust management strategies based on feedback and changing needs. Continuously refine your approach to ensure it aligns with the evolving dynamics of your multigenerational workforce.

By effectively managing and motivating a diverse team, you can leverage the strengths of different generations to drive innovation and achieve organizational goals. Embracing generational diversity and implementing tailored strategies will enhance collaboration, creativity, and overall performance.

# Chapter 13: Enhancing Personal Leadership

## Developing Personal Leadership Skills

Improving personal leadership skills is crucial for effective leadership and achieving career goals. Here's how to enhance your individual leadership abilities:

1. **Self-Awareness and Reflection:**

• Assess Strengths and Weaknesses: Conduct self-assessments to identify your leadership strengths and areas for improvement. Use tools such as personality assessments, 360-degree feedback, and self-reflection exercises.

• Set Personal Development Goals: Based on your self-assessment, set specific, measurable goals for improving your leadership skills. Focus on areas that align with your career aspirations and organizational needs.

2. **Develop Key Leadership Competencies:**

• Enhance Communication Skills: Improve your ability to communicate effectively by practicing active listening, clear articulation, and constructive feedback. Develop skills for both verbal and non-verbal communication.

• Strengthen Decision-Making Abilities: Enhance your decision-making skills by analyzing situations critically, considering multiple perspectives, and evaluating potential outcomes. Practice making informed and timely decisions.

• Build Emotional Intelligence: Develop emotional intelligence to better understand and manage your emotions and those of others. This includes improving self-regulation, empathy, and interpersonal relationships.

3. **Cultivate Leadership Behaviors:**

• Lead by Example: Model the behaviors and values you expect from others. Demonstrate integrity, accountability, and commitment in your actions and decisions.

• Empower and Inspire Others: Focus on empowering and inspiring your team by providing support, recognizing achievements, and fostering a positive work environment. Encourage and mentor others to achieve their full potential.

4. **Seek Feedback and Coaching:**

• Request Constructive Feedback: Solicit feedback from colleagues, mentors, and team members to gain insights into your leadership performance. Use this feedback to make targeted improvements.

• Engage in Coaching: Work with a leadership coach to receive personalized guidance and support. A coach can help you identify areas for growth, develop action plans, and overcome challenges.

5. **Build Resilience and Adaptability:**

• Develop Coping Strategies: Strengthen your ability to handle stress and setbacks by developing effective coping strategies. Practice mindfulness, stress management techniques, and resilience-building activities.

• Adapt to Change: Enhance your adaptability by embracing change and being open to new approaches. Develop skills to navigate uncertainty and guide your team through transitions.

**The Importance of Continuous Learning**

Ongoing education and personal growth are vital for sustaining effective leadership. Here's why continuous learning is essential and how to incorporate it into your leadership journey:

1. **Stay Current with Industry Trends:**

    • Monitor Industry Developments: Keep abreast of the latest trends, technologies, and best practices in your industry. This knowledge will help you make informed decisions and stay competitive.

    • Attend Conferences and Seminars: Participate in industry conferences, seminars, and webinars to gain new insights and network with other professionals. These events provide valuable learning opportunities and exposure to emerging trends.

2. **Pursue Professional Development:**

    • Enroll in Leadership Programs: Take advantage of leadership development programs and courses that offer advanced training in key leadership areas. These programs can enhance your skills and expand your knowledge base.

    • Obtain Certifications: Consider earning certifications in relevant areas, such as project management, strategic planning, or change management. Certifications can add credibility to your leadership expertise and open new opportunities.

3. **Engage in Self-Directed Learning:**

    • Read Books and Articles: Stay informed by reading books, articles, and research papers on leadership, management, and personal development. Choose materials that challenge your thinking and offer practical insights.

    • Participate in Online Learning: Explore online learning platforms and courses that cover a wide range of topics related to leadership and personal growth. Online learning offers flexibility and access to diverse resources.

4. **Reflect and Apply Learning:**

    • Practice New Skills: Apply new knowledge and skills in your daily leadership activities. Experiment with different approaches and techniques to see what works best for you and your team.

    • Reflect on Experiences: Regularly reflect on your learning experiences and their impact on your leadership effectiveness. Assess what you've learned and how it has influenced your leadership style.

5. **Foster a Growth Mindset:**

• Embrace Challenges: Approach challenges as opportunities for growth and development. A growth mindset will help you remain resilient and motivated in the face of obstacles.

• Seek Opportunities for Improvement: Continuously seek ways to improve your leadership skills and knowledge. Be open to feedback and willing to make adjustments based on your experiences.

6. **Build a Support Network:**

• Connect with Peers and Mentors: Build a network of peers, mentors, and advisors who can provide support, guidance, and inspiration. Engage with individuals who can offer diverse perspectives and insights.

• Participate in Professional Groups: Join professional organizations and leadership communities to expand your network and gain access to valuable resources and learning opportunities.

By focusing on personal leadership development and embracing continuous learning, you can enhance your effectiveness as a leader and drive your career success. Investing in your growth will help you adapt to evolving challenges, lead with confidence, and achieve your leadership goals.

## Chapter 14: Future Leadership Strategies

### Anticipating Future Trends

To effectively navigate and lead in the future, it's crucial to anticipate emerging trends and adapt your strategies accordingly. Here's how to identify and prepare for future trends:

1. **Conduct Environmental Scanning:**

• Monitor Industry Developments: Regularly review industry reports, market analyses, and technological advancements. Stay informed about changes that could impact your organization and industry.

• Track Emerging Trends: Identify and analyze emerging trends and technologies that could influence your sector. Consider factors such as demographic shifts, economic changes, and advancements in technology.

2. **Analyze Future Scenarios:**

• Develop Scenario Planning: Use scenario planning to explore different future scenarios and their potential impact on your organization. Create multiple scenarios based on varying assumptions and uncertainties.

• Evaluate Potential Impacts: Assess how each scenario might affect your business operations, strategies, and goals. Identify opportunities and risks associated with each potential future.

3. **Leverage Data and Analytics:**

• Utilize Big Data: Harness big data and analytics tools to gain insights into future trends and patterns. Use data-driven approaches to inform your strategic planning and decision-making.

• Analyze Market Signals: Track market signals and indicators that suggest emerging trends. This could include shifts in consumer behavior, investment patterns, and technological innovations.

4. **Engage with Thought Leaders:**

• Connect with Experts: Engage with industry thought leaders, futurists, and experts to gain insights into future trends and developments. Attend conferences, webinars, and discussions to gather diverse perspectives.

• Join Professional Networks: Participate in professional networks and forums focused on future trends and innovation. These networks provide valuable information and opportunities for collaboration.

5. **Foster a Culture of Innovation:**

• Encourage Experimentation: Promote a culture that encourages experimentation and innovation. Support initiatives that explore new ideas and technologies, and be open to unconventional approaches.

• Invest in Research and Development: Allocate resources to research and development activities that explore emerging trends and technologies. Invest in projects that have the potential to drive future growth.

**Preparing for Change**

Effective preparation for future changes is essential for maintaining organizational resilience and adaptability. Here's how to develop strategies to prepare for potential changes in the business environment:

1. **Develop a Flexible Strategy:**

    • Build Agility into Your Strategy: Create a flexible strategy that can adapt to changing conditions. Incorporate elements such as contingency planning and scenario analysis to accommodate unforeseen developments.

    • Review and Update Plans Regularly: Regularly review and update your strategic plans to reflect new information and changes in the environment. Ensure that your plans remain relevant and aligned with current trends.

2. **Strengthen Organizational Resilience:**

    • Build a Resilient Culture: Foster a culture of resilience within your organization by encouraging adaptability and continuous learning. Equip employees with the skills and mindset to handle change effectively.

    • Develop Crisis Management Capabilities: Enhance your organization's crisis management capabilities by establishing robust response plans and conducting regular simulations. Prepare your team to respond quickly and effectively to disruptions.

3. **Enhance Change Management Processes:**

    • Implement Change Management Frameworks: Use change management frameworks and methodologies to guide your organization through transitions. Apply structured approaches to manage the impact of change on employees and operations.

    • Communicate Effectively: Ensure clear and consistent communication throughout the change process. Provide regular updates, address concerns, and involve employees in the change initiatives.

4. **Invest in Technology and Infrastructure:**

    • Adopt New Technologies: Invest in technologies that support future growth and enhance operational efficiency. Stay current with technological advancements that could provide a competitive advantage.

    • Upgrade Infrastructure: Ensure that your organizational infrastructure is capable of supporting future changes. Upgrade systems and processes to accommodate evolving needs and requirements.

### 5. Cultivate Strategic Partnerships:

• Form Strategic Alliances: Develop strategic partnerships and alliances with other organizations, institutions, and stakeholders. Collaborate on initiatives that address future challenges and opportunities.

• Engage with Ecosystem Partners: Participate in industry ecosystems and networks that provide insights into future trends and facilitate collaboration. Leverage partnerships to enhance your organization's capabilities.

### 6. Foster Leadership Development:

• Prepare Future Leaders: Invest in leadership development programs that prepare future leaders for upcoming challenges. Equip them with the skills and knowledge needed to navigate complex and evolving environments.

• Promote Continuous Learning: Encourage continuous learning and professional development for all employees. Support their growth to ensure they are equipped to handle future changes and innovations.

### 7. Monitor and Evaluate Progress:

• Track Implementation of Strategies: Monitor the implementation of strategies and initiatives aimed at preparing for future changes. Assess their effectiveness and make adjustments as needed.

• Evaluate Outcomes and Impact: Regularly evaluate the outcomes and impact of your preparations for change. Use feedback and performance metrics to refine your approach and improve future readiness.

By anticipating future trends and preparing for change, you can position your organization to thrive in an evolving business landscape. Developing flexible strategies, enhancing resilience, and investing in leadership and technology will enable you to navigate future challenges and seize emerging opportunities.

# Chapter 15: Enhancing Cross-Cultural Collaboration

## Achieving Effective Collaboration

To foster effective collaboration among global and diverse teams, it's essential to implement strategies that bridge cultural gaps and facilitate seamless teamwork. Here's how to enhance collaboration across cultures:

1. **Build a Shared Vision and Goals:**

    • Define Common Objectives: Establish clear, shared objectives that align with the overall goals of the team or organization. Ensure that all members understand and are committed to these objectives.

    • Create a Unified Mission Statement: Develop a mission statement that reflects the collective values and purpose of the team. Use this statement to guide decision-making and align efforts.

2. **Promote Open Communication:**

    • Encourage Transparent Dialogue: Foster an environment where open and honest communication is encouraged. Create channels for team members to express their ideas, concerns, and feedback.

    • Use Common Language: Ensure that communication is conducted in a language that is understood by all team members. Provide translation or interpretation services if necessary.

3. **Leverage Technology for Collaboration:**

    • Adopt Collaboration Tools: Utilize digital collaboration tools and platforms that facilitate communication and coordination among team members, regardless of their location.

    • Implement Virtual Meeting Solutions: Use virtual meeting technologies to conduct regular meetings and discussions. Ensure that these solutions are accessible and user-friendly for all team members.

### 4. Foster Team-Building Activities:

• Organize Cross-Cultural Team-Building Events: Plan activities that bring team members together and promote bonding. Activities could include workshops, team challenges, and social events.

• Encourage Informal Interactions: Create opportunities for team members to interact informally, such as through virtual coffee breaks or social networks, to build relationships and trust.

### 5. Recognize and Celebrate Contributions:

• Acknowledge Achievements: Recognize and celebrate the contributions and achievements of team members from different cultural backgrounds. Use various recognition methods, such as awards, public acknowledgment, or team celebrations.

• Promote Inclusivity: Ensure that recognition and rewards are inclusive and reflective of the diverse contributions of the team. Avoid favoring one culture or group over another.

## Managing Cultural Differences

Effectively managing cultural differences is key to overcoming challenges and fostering a collaborative environment. Here's how to address and leverage cultural diversity:

### 1. Understand Cultural Norms and Values:

• Conduct Cultural Assessments: Assess the cultural norms, values, and practices of team members. This understanding helps in addressing potential misunderstandings and fostering mutual respect.

• Provide Cultural Training: Offer cultural awareness training to team members to increase their understanding of different cultural perspectives and practices. This training should cover topics such as communication styles, etiquette, and decision-making.

### 2. Address Cultural Misunderstandings:

• Promote Open Dialogue: Encourage team members to discuss cultural differences openly and address any misunderstandings that arise. Provide a safe space for such discussions.

• Implement Mediation Processes: Establish processes for resolving conflicts and misunderstandings that stem from cultural differences. Utilize mediation and conflict resolution techniques to address issues constructively.

3. **Adapt Leadership Styles:**

• Be Culturally Sensitive: Adapt your leadership style to accommodate the cultural preferences and expectations of your team members. Recognize that different cultures may have varying approaches to leadership and collaboration.

• Flexibility in Approach: Be flexible in your approach to managing and motivating team members. Tailor your strategies to suit the diverse needs and preferences of your team.

4. **Foster Inclusion and Equity:**

• Promote Inclusive Practices: Implement practices that ensure all team members feel included and valued. This includes equitable participation in decision-making, access to resources, and opportunities for advancement.

• Address Bias and Discrimination: Actively address any instances of bias or discrimination within the team. Implement policies and procedures to prevent and address such issues.

5. **Encourage Cultural Exchange:**

• Facilitate Knowledge Sharing: Create opportunities for team members to share their cultural knowledge and experiences. This exchange can enhance understanding and appreciation of different perspectives.

• Organize Cultural Events: Host cultural events and celebrations that highlight the diverse backgrounds of team members. These events can promote cultural awareness and strengthen team cohesion.

6. **Leverage Diverse Perspectives:**

• Utilize Diverse Insights: Harness the diverse perspectives and insights of team members to drive innovation and problem-solving. Encourage team members to contribute their unique viewpoints and ideas.

• Integrate Best Practices: Incorporate best practices from different cultures into your team's processes and strategies. This integration can lead to improved practices and outcomes.

7. **Monitor and Evaluate Collaboration Efforts:**

• Assess Collaboration Effectiveness: Regularly evaluate the effectiveness of collaboration efforts and strategies. Use feedback and performance metrics to identify areas for improvement.

• Adjust Strategies as Needed: Be prepared to adjust collaboration strategies based on feedback and evolving team dynamics. Continuously refine your approach to enhance cross-cultural collaboration.

By implementing these strategies, you can enhance cross-cultural collaboration, manage cultural differences effectively, and create a more cohesive and productive global team. Embracing cultural diversity and fostering an inclusive environment will lead to greater innovation, improved team performance, and successful outcomes.

## Chapter 16: Strategic Analysis and Planning

**Analyzing the Strategic Environment**

Understanding the internal and external environment of an organization is crucial for developing effective strategies. Here's a detailed approach to strategic analysis:

1. **Conduct Internal Analysis:**

 • Assess Organizational Resources and Capabilities: Evaluate your organization's resources, including financial, human, and technological assets. Analyze capabilities such as operational efficiency, innovation, and customer service.

 • Identify Strengths and Weaknesses: Use tools like SWOT (Strengths, Weaknesses, Opportunities, Threats) analysis to identify internal strengths and weaknesses. Focus on areas that impact your competitive advantage and operational effectiveness.

 • Evaluate Organizational Performance: Review performance metrics and benchmarks to assess how well your organization is meeting its goals. Analyze financial statements, market share, and other performance indicators.

2. **Conduct External Analysis:**

 • Analyze Market and Industry Trends: Examine trends in your industry, including market growth, competitive dynamics, and technological advancements. Use tools like PESTEL (Political, Economic, Social, Technological, Environmental, Legal) analysis to understand external factors.

 • Assess Competitive Landscape: Identify and evaluate key competitors, their strengths and weaknesses, and their market positioning. Use Porter's Five Forces model to assess competitive pressures and potential threats.

 • Understand Customer Needs and Preferences: Analyze customer demographics, preferences, and behaviors. Conduct market research, surveys, and focus groups to gather insights into customer needs and expectations.

### 3. Evaluate Strategic Position:

•   Review Strategic Objectives: Assess the alignment of current strategic objectives with the organization's vision and mission. Ensure that objectives are clear, measurable, and achievable.

•   Identify Opportunities and Threats: Use the insights from internal and external analysis to identify strategic opportunities and threats. Focus on areas where the organization can capitalize on opportunities or mitigate potential risks.

**Developing Effective Strategies**

Based on the analysis, develop strategies that address both internal capabilities and external opportunities and threats. Here's how to create and implement effective strategies:

### 1. Formulate Strategic Goals:

•   Set Clear and Achievable Goals: Develop specific, measurable, attainable, relevant, and time-bound (SMART) goals that align with your strategic vision. Ensure that goals address key areas of focus identified during the analysis.

•   Prioritize Strategic Objectives: Prioritize strategic objectives based on their impact and feasibility. Allocate resources and efforts to the most critical areas that will drive success.

### 2. Develop Strategic Options:

•   Explore Alternative Strategies: Generate and evaluate different strategic options based on the analysis. Consider various approaches such as market expansion, diversification, cost leadership, or differentiation.

•   Assess Feasibility and Risks: Analyze the feasibility and potential risks associated with each strategic option. Evaluate factors such as resource requirements, financial implications, and implementation challenges.

### 3. Select and Implement Strategies:

•   Choose the Best Strategy: Select the most effective strategy based on the analysis and evaluation of options. Ensure that the chosen strategy aligns with the organization's goals and capabilities.

•   Develop an Implementation Plan: Create a detailed implementation plan outlining key actions, responsibilities, timelines, and resources required. Ensure that the plan includes mechanisms for monitoring and evaluating progress.

### 4. Monitor and Adjust Strategies:

• Track Performance and Progress: Regularly monitor the implementation of strategies and track performance against established goals. Use performance metrics and feedback to assess effectiveness.

• Adapt and Refine Strategies: Be prepared to adapt and refine strategies based on performance data, changing conditions, and new insights. Continuously review and adjust strategies to ensure alignment with organizational goals and external factors.

### 5. Foster Strategic Alignment:

• Ensure Organizational Alignment: Align organizational structure, processes, and resources with the strategic goals. Ensure that all departments and teams are working towards common objectives.

• Communicate Strategies Effectively: Communicate the strategic plan and its objectives to all stakeholders. Ensure that employees understand their roles and contributions to the strategy.

### 6. Leverage Strategic Tools and Frameworks:

• Use Strategic Planning Tools: Utilize tools such as the Balanced Scorecard, SWOT analysis, and scenario planning to enhance strategic planning and decision-making.

• Incorporate Benchmarking: Benchmark against industry standards and best practices to identify areas for improvement and ensure competitive positioning.

By conducting thorough strategic analysis and developing well-informed strategies, organizations can navigate complex environments, seize opportunities, and address challenges effectively. Strategic planning is an ongoing process that requires continuous assessment and adaptation to ensure long-term success and growth.

# Chapter 17: Building Sustainable Strategies

**Integrating Sustainability**

Incorporating sustainability into leadership strategies is crucial for long-term success and positive impact. Here's how to embed sustainability principles into your strategic planning:

1. **Define Sustainability Objectives:**

    • Set Clear Sustainability Goals: Establish specific, measurable, and time-bound sustainability goals that align with your organization's mission and values. Focus on areas such as environmental impact, social responsibility, and economic viability.

    • Align with Global Standards: Ensure that your sustainability objectives align with global standards and frameworks, such as the United Nations Sustainable Development Goals (SDGs) or industry-specific sustainability certifications.

2. **Embed Sustainability into Strategic Vision:**

    • Incorporate Sustainability into Mission and Vision: Integrate sustainability into your organization's mission and vision statements. Emphasize your commitment to environmental and social responsibility in your strategic direction.

    • Communicate Sustainability Commitment: Clearly communicate your sustainability goals and commitments to stakeholders, including employees, customers, investors, and partners.

3. **Develop Sustainable Business Models:**

    • Innovate for Sustainability: Explore and implement business models that prioritize sustainability. Consider models such as circular economy, green innovation, and sustainable supply chains.

    • Evaluate Environmental and Social Impact: Assess the environmental and social impact of your business operations and products. Use tools such as life cycle assessment (LCA) to measure and manage impacts.

### 4. Integrate Sustainability into Strategic Planning:

•   Incorporate Sustainability into Strategy Formulation: Ensure that sustainability considerations are integrated into the formulation of strategic goals and initiatives. Evaluate how sustainability can enhance or drive strategic opportunities.

•   Develop a Sustainability Strategy: Create a dedicated sustainability strategy that outlines specific initiatives, targets, and performance metrics. Ensure that this strategy complements and supports your overall business strategy.

**Implementing Sustainable Initiatives**

Integrating sustainability into daily operations involves practical steps to ensure that sustainability principles are reflected in everyday practices. Here's how to implement sustainable initiatives effectively:

### 1. Embed Sustainability in Operations:

•   Optimize Resource Use: Implement practices to reduce resource consumption and waste. Focus on energy efficiency, water conservation, and sustainable materials in your operations.

•   Adopt Green Technologies: Invest in and adopt green technologies and processes that minimize environmental impact. Examples include renewable energy sources, waste reduction technologies, and eco-friendly packaging.

### 2. Engage Stakeholders in Sustainability Efforts:

•   Involve Employees: Engage employees in sustainability initiatives by fostering a culture of environmental and social responsibility. Provide training and resources to help employees contribute to sustainability goals.

•   Collaborate with Partners: Work with suppliers, partners, and other stakeholders to promote sustainability throughout your value chain. Encourage collaboration on sustainability projects and initiatives.

### 3. Monitor and Report on Sustainability Performance:

• Track Progress: Regularly monitor and measure the performance of sustainability initiatives using established metrics and key performance indicators (KPIs). Evaluate progress towards sustainability goals and targets.

• Report Transparently: Provide transparent and regular reports on your sustainability performance to stakeholders. Use sustainability reporting frameworks such as the Global Reporting Initiative (GRI) or the Sustainability Accounting Standards Board (SASB) standards.

### 4. Foster a Culture of Continuous Improvement:

• Encourage Innovation: Promote a culture of continuous improvement by encouraging innovation and new ideas related to sustainability. Support initiatives that drive further advancements in sustainable practices.

• Solicit Feedback: Gather feedback from employees, customers, and other stakeholders on sustainability initiatives. Use this feedback to refine and enhance your sustainability efforts.

### 5. Evaluate and Adjust Strategies:

• Assess Impact: Regularly evaluate the impact of your sustainability initiatives on your organization's goals and overall performance. Identify areas for improvement and adjust strategies as needed.

• Adapt to Changes: Stay informed about evolving sustainability trends, regulations, and best practices. Adapt your strategies to address new challenges and opportunities in the sustainability landscape.

### 6. Promote Sustainable Products and Services:

• Develop Sustainable Offerings: Design and market products and services that prioritize sustainability. Focus on features such as energy efficiency, recyclable materials, and ethical sourcing.

• Educate Customers: Educate customers about the sustainability benefits of your products and services. Use marketing and communication strategies to highlight your commitment to sustainable practices.

By embedding sustainability into your strategic vision and implementing practical initiatives, you can create a more resilient and responsible organization. Sustainable strategies not only contribute to positive environmental and social outcomes but also enhance your organization's long-term success and competitive advantage.

# Chapter 18: Leading Through Innovation

## Fostering Continuous Innovation

Developing a culture of continuous innovation requires strategic leadership and a supportive environment. Here's how to create and sustain innovation within your organization:

1. **Create an Innovation-Friendly Culture:**

    • Encourage Creativity: Foster an environment where creativity is valued and encouraged. Support initiatives that allow employees to explore new ideas and think outside the box.

    • Support Risk-Taking: Promote a culture that embraces risk-taking and experimentation. Encourage teams to pursue innovative projects without fear of failure.

2. **Develop an Innovation Strategy:**

    • Align Innovation with Business Goals: Ensure that your innovation strategy is aligned with your organization's overall business goals and objectives. Focus on areas where innovation can drive significant value.

    • Allocate Resources for Innovation: Invest in resources, including time, budget, and talent, dedicated to innovation efforts. Ensure that teams have the tools and support needed to explore and develop new ideas.

3. **Implement Structured Innovation Processes:**

    • Establish Innovation Frameworks: Use structured frameworks and methodologies, such as design thinking or agile development, to guide innovation efforts. These processes help in systematically developing and implementing new ideas.

    • Encourage Cross-Functional Collaboration: Promote collaboration across different departments and functions to leverage diverse perspectives and expertise. Facilitate brainstorming sessions and collaborative projects.

4. **Promote Learning and Knowledge Sharing:**

• Facilitate Knowledge Exchange: Create platforms and opportunities for employees to share knowledge and best practices related to innovation. Encourage participation in workshops, seminars, and industry conferences.

• Invest in Training and Development: Provide training programs that enhance employees' skills in innovation-related areas, such as creative problem-solving, project management, and technology.

5. **Monitor and Evaluate Innovation Efforts:**

• Track Innovation Metrics: Use metrics and key performance indicators (KPIs) to measure the effectiveness of innovation initiatives. Monitor progress and assess the impact of new ideas on business performance.

• Review and Refine Strategies: Regularly review innovation strategies and processes to identify areas for improvement. Make adjustments based on feedback and performance data.

## Handling Failure as a Learning Opportunity

Failure is an inherent part of the innovation process and can provide valuable lessons. Here's how to manage failure constructively and use it as a springboard for future innovation:

1. **Create a Safe Environment for Failure:**

• Encourage Open Dialogue: Promote a culture where failure is viewed as a learning opportunity rather than a setback. Encourage open discussions about failures and the lessons learned.

• Avoid Blame: Focus on understanding the root causes of failure rather than assigning blame. Support employees in analyzing and addressing issues constructively.

2. **Analyze and Learn from Failures:**

• Conduct Post-Mortem Reviews: After a failure, conduct thorough post-mortem reviews to analyze what went wrong and why. Identify key factors that contributed to the failure and areas for improvement.

• Document Lessons Learned: Capture and document the lessons learned from failures. Share these insights with the team to avoid repeating the same mistakes and to improve future innovation efforts.

### 3. Encourage Iteration and Improvement:

- Promote Iterative Development: Adopt iterative development approaches, such as rapid prototyping or incremental improvements, to refine ideas based on feedback and learning from failures.

- Support Continuous Improvement: Encourage teams to continuously improve and iterate on their ideas. Use failures as opportunities to enhance processes and outcomes.

### 4. Celebrate Resilience and Perseverance:

- Recognize Efforts and Resilience: Celebrate the efforts of individuals and teams who demonstrate resilience and perseverance in the face of failure. Acknowledge their contributions and commitment to innovation.

- Inspire a Growth Mindset: Promote a growth mindset within the organization, where challenges and failures are seen as opportunities for growth and development.

### 5. Implement Feedback Loops:

- Establish Feedback Mechanisms: Create feedback loops to gather insights from stakeholders, including customers, employees, and partners. Use this feedback to make informed decisions and improve innovation efforts.

- Incorporate Feedback into Processes: Integrate feedback into innovation processes to refine and enhance ideas. Ensure that feedback is used constructively to drive positive changes.

### 6. Foster Resilient Leadership:

- Model Resilience: Demonstrate resilience and a positive attitude towards failure as a leader. Show how setbacks are managed and learned from, setting an example for the team.

- Provide Support and Guidance: Offer support and guidance to teams dealing with failure. Help them navigate challenges and maintain focus on long-term innovation goals.

By fostering a culture of continuous innovation and handling failure constructively, organizations can drive sustained growth and creativity. Embracing innovation and learning from failures not only enhances organizational capabilities but also positions the organization for long-term success and competitive advantage.

# Chapter 19: Case Studies and Inspiring Experiences

**Inspiring Success Stories**

Examining real-world examples of successful leadership and transformative change provides valuable insights and inspiration. Here's how to present and analyze these stories effectively:

1. **Showcase Notable Success Stories:**

    • Highlight Diverse Industries: Present success stories from a range of industries and sectors to demonstrate the versatility of effective leadership. Include examples from technology, healthcare, finance, and non-profit organizations.

    • Focus on Key Achievements: Detail the key achievements and milestones of each success story. Emphasize the significant impact of leadership on organizational performance and transformation.

2. **Detail Leadership Approaches:**

    • Describe Leadership Strategies: Outline the leadership strategies and approaches used by successful leaders. Highlight their vision, decision-making processes, and how they navigated challenges.

    • Explore Innovation and Change: Discuss how these leaders drove innovation and managed change. Explain the specific actions and decisions that led to successful outcomes.

3. **Illustrate Organizational Impact:**

    • Showcase Transformative Outcomes: Illustrate the transformative outcomes achieved by these leaders. Provide quantitative and qualitative evidence of the impact on the organization, such as increased revenue, market share, or employee satisfaction.

    • Highlight Long-Term Benefits: Discuss the long-term benefits and sustainable changes resulting from the leadership efforts. Emphasize how these changes positioned the organization for future success.

4. **Extract Lessons Learned:**

    • Identify Key Takeaways: Identify and summarize the key takeaways from each success story. Highlight the principles and practices that contributed to the leaders' achievements.

    • Relate to Broader Context: Relate the lessons learned to broader leadership and organizational contexts. Explain how these insights can be applied to other organizations and leadership situations.

**Analyzing Case Studies**

Analyzing case studies involves a deep dive into successful experiences to understand the factors contributing to their success. Here's how to analyze and learn from case studies effectively:

1. **Conduct In-Depth Analysis:**

    • Review Case Study Components: Analyze the components of the case study, including the organizational context, leadership approach, strategies implemented, and outcomes achieved.

    • Evaluate Decision-Making Processes: Examine the decision-making processes used by leaders in the case studies. Assess how decisions were made and the rationale behind them.

2. **Assess Organizational Practices:**

    • Analyze Strategic Initiatives: Evaluate the strategic initiatives and actions taken by the organization. Assess how these initiatives aligned with the organization's goals and objectives.

    • Review Implementation Challenges: Identify and review the challenges encountered during implementation. Analyze how these challenges were addressed and overcome.

3. **Identify Success Factors:**

    • Pinpoint Key Success Factors: Identify the key factors that contributed to the success of the case studies. These may include effective leadership, innovative strategies, strong organizational culture, or market positioning.

    • Assess Impact of Leadership: Analyze the impact of leadership on achieving successful outcomes. Consider how leadership qualities, vision, and actions influenced the organization's success.

4. **Draw Lessons and Best Practices:**

    • Extract Practical Lessons: Extract practical lessons and best practices from the case studies. Consider how these lessons can be applied to different contexts and leadership scenarios.

    • Develop Actionable Insights: Develop actionable insights based on the case study analysis. Create recommendations for applying these insights to enhance leadership effectiveness and drive organizational success.

**5. Share Insights and Recommendations:**

• Communicate Findings: Share the insights and recommendations derived from the case study analysis with relevant stakeholders. Use clear and concise communication to convey the value of the lessons learned.

• Provide Guidance for Application: Offer guidance on how to apply the insights and best practices to other organizations or leadership situations. Provide practical examples and steps for implementation.

**6. Incorporate Feedback and Continuous Learning:**

• Seek Feedback: Gather feedback from stakeholders on the case study analysis and insights shared. Use this feedback to refine and improve the analysis process.

• Promote Continuous Learning: Encourage continuous learning and exploration of additional case studies. Foster a culture of learning from successful experiences and applying lessons to drive ongoing improvement.

By showcasing inspiring success stories and conducting thorough case study analyses, organizations and leaders can gain valuable insights into effective leadership and transformative change. These real-world examples and lessons learned provide a roadmap for achieving success and driving innovation in diverse contexts.

# Chapter 20: Continuous Evolution as a Leader

**Personal Growth Strategies**

Sustaining growth and development as a leader requires intentional effort and a commitment to personal improvement. Here's how to cultivate ongoing evolution in your leadership journey:

**1. Commit to Lifelong Learning:**

• Pursue Continuous Education: Engage in continuous learning through formal education, such as advanced degrees, certifications, and workshops. Stay updated on the latest trends and advancements in your field.

• Attend Industry Conferences and Seminars: Participate in industry conferences, seminars, and webinars to gain new insights and network with other professionals. These events provide opportunities for learning and professional development.

**2. Seek Feedback and Coaching:**

- Request Regular Feedback: Actively seek feedback from peers, mentors, and team members. Use this feedback to identify areas for improvement and to gain different perspectives on your leadership style.

- Engage with a Coach or Mentor: Work with a coach or mentor who can provide guidance, support, and constructive feedback. A coach or mentor can help you set goals, overcome challenges, and develop new skills.

**3. Reflect and Self-Assess:**

- Practice Self-Reflection: Regularly reflect on your leadership experiences, successes, and challenges. Use journaling or self-assessment tools to analyze your growth and identify areas for development.

- Evaluate Personal Strengths and Weaknesses: Conduct a thorough self-assessment to understand your strengths and weaknesses as a leader. Use this understanding to focus on areas where you can enhance your capabilities.

**4. Set and Pursue Personal Development Goals:**

- Establish Clear Goals: Set specific, measurable, achievable, relevant, and time-bound (SMART) goals for your personal and professional development. These goals should align with your long-term vision and aspirations.

- Create a Development Plan: Develop a personalized growth plan outlining the steps and resources needed to achieve your goals. Include milestones and timelines to track your progress.

**5. Embrace Challenges and Change:**

- Take on New Challenges: Seek out and embrace new challenges and opportunities that push you beyond your comfort zone. Tackling complex problems and leading new initiatives can accelerate your growth.

- Adapt to Change: Stay flexible and adaptable in the face of change. Develop the ability to lead through uncertainty and guide your team through evolving circumstances.

**Developing and Implementing Personal Growth Plans**

Creating and executing a personal growth plan involves strategic planning and consistent effort. Here's how to effectively develop and implement your growth plan:

1. **Assess Current Skills and Knowledge:**

    • Conduct a Skills Inventory: Identify and evaluate your current skills, knowledge, and experiences. Determine which areas are strong and which need further development.

    • Identify Growth Opportunities: Based on your assessment, identify opportunities for growth and development. Focus on areas that will enhance your leadership effectiveness and support your career goals.

2. **Design a Comprehensive Growth Plan:**

    • Outline Development Activities: Create a detailed plan that includes specific activities and resources for achieving your growth goals. This may include training programs, reading materials, mentorship, or project involvement.

    • Set Milestones and Deadlines: Establish milestones and deadlines for achieving your growth objectives. Break down larger goals into manageable steps and track your progress regularly.

3. **Implement the Growth Plan:**

    • Take Action: Begin implementing your growth plan by engaging in the identified development activities. Stay committed to your plan and make adjustments as needed to stay on track.

    • Monitor Progress: Regularly review your progress against the established milestones and deadlines. Adjust your plan as necessary to address any challenges or changes in priorities.

4. **Evaluate and Adjust:**

    • Assess Outcomes: Periodically evaluate the outcomes of your growth plan. Determine whether you have achieved your goals and how the development activities have impacted your leadership capabilities.

    • Refine the Plan: Based on your evaluation, refine and adjust your growth plan to address any gaps or new areas of focus. Continuously adapt your plan to align with your evolving goals and circumstances.

### 5. Celebrate Achievements and Reflect:

- Acknowledge Successes: Celebrate your achievements and milestones reached in your personal growth journey. Recognize the progress you have made and the skills you have developed.

- Reflect on Lessons Learned: Reflect on the lessons learned throughout your growth process. Use these insights to guide your future development and leadership practices.

### 6. Share Knowledge and Mentor Others:

- Mentor and Coach Others: Share your experiences and knowledge with others by mentoring or coaching emerging leaders. Providing guidance to others can enhance your own growth and reinforce your learning.

By committing to continuous personal growth and developing a strategic plan for self-improvement, you can enhance your leadership capabilities and achieve long-term success. Ongoing development is essential for staying relevant and effective in an ever-evolving leadership landscape.

## Conclusion

### Summary of Key Points

In this book, we have delved into the essential components of effective leadership in the modern era. Here's a summary of the core ideas and strategies covered:

### 1. Vision for the Future:

- The importance of establishing a clear, inspiring vision to guide your organization.
- Techniques for anticipating future trends and incorporating them into your strategic planning.

### 2. Fostering Innovation:

- Strategies for nurturing a culture of creativity and continuous improvement.
- Methods for motivating teams and implementing innovative ideas successfully.

3. **Navigating Digital Transformation:**
   - Best practices for integrating digital technologies into your leadership strategy.
   - Approaches for overcoming challenges associated with digital change.

4. **Strategic Planning for Change:**
   - Developing comprehensive plans to manage organizational change.
   - Effective resource allocation to support successful implementation of change initiatives.

5. **Building a Strong Team:**
   - Techniques for assembling and managing high-performing, diverse teams.
   - Strategies for leading and supporting teams from various backgrounds and experiences.

6. **Ethical Leadership and Social Responsibility:**
   - The role of ethical behavior in building trust and a positive organizational reputation.
   - Integrating social responsibility into your leadership approach.

7. **Effective Communication:**
   - Enhancing communication skills to engage and inform stakeholders effectively.
   - Managing misinformation and maintaining transparency during crises.

8. **Cultural Change Management:**
   - Techniques for transforming organizational culture to support new initiatives.
   - Measuring the impact of cultural changes on performance and morale.

9. **Crisis Leadership:**
   - Strategies for managing crises and maintaining effective communication during challenging times.
   - Ensuring resilience and stability in the face of adversity.

10. **Performance Measurement:**
    - Setting and evaluating key performance indicators to assess success and areas for improvement.
    - Analyzing outcomes and making data-driven adjustments to leadership strategies.

11. **Generational Innovation:**

- Leveraging generational diversity to drive innovation and address varying perspectives.
- Managing and motivating multi-generational teams effectively.

12. **Personal Leadership Development:**

- Strategies for ongoing personal growth and skill enhancement as a leader.
- The importance of continuous learning and self-assessment.

13. **Future Leadership Strategies:**

- Anticipating future trends and preparing for potential changes in the business environment.
- Developing flexible strategies to adapt to evolving leadership challenges.

14. **Cross-Cultural Collaboration:**

- Facilitating effective collaboration across different cultures and managing cultural differences.
- Building a cohesive global team and fostering international cooperation.

15. **Strategic Analysis and Planning:**

- Analyzing internal and external factors to develop effective strategies.
- Crafting strategies based on comprehensive environmental analysis.

16. **Sustainable Leadership:**

- Integrating sustainability principles into leadership practices.
- Implementing initiatives that promote long-term environmental and social responsibility.

17. **Innovation Leadership:**

- Supporting continuous innovation and learning from failure.
- Developing strategies to maintain an innovative mindset and approach.

### 18. Case Studies and Inspiration:

- Drawing insights from successful case studies and analyzing key factors behind their success.

- Applying lessons learned to enhance leadership practices and drive transformative change.

### 19. Continuous Personal Evolution:

- Committing to lifelong learning and personal development.

- Developing and executing growth plans to sustain leadership effectiveness.

**Guidance for Next Steps**

To effectively apply the strategies and insights gained from this book, consider the following actionable steps:

### 1. Assess and Reflect:

- Evaluate your current leadership practices and identify areas for improvement based on the key strategies discussed.

- Reflect on your personal growth and development goals, and align them with the insights from the book.

### 2. Develop a Plan:

- Create a detailed action plan incorporating the strategies and best practices outlined in the book.

- Set clear objectives, milestones, and timelines for implementing these strategies within your organization.

### 3. Engage Your Team:

- Communicate your vision and plans to your team, and involve them in the process of implementing changes.

- Encourage feedback and collaboration to ensure buy-in and foster a supportive environment.

**4. Monitor and Adjust:**

- Regularly review the progress of your initiatives and measure outcomes against your objectives.
- Make necessary adjustments based on feedback and performance data to stay on track and achieve desired results.

**5. Commit to Continuous Learning:**

- Continue your personal development journey by pursuing additional learning opportunities and staying updated on industry trends.
- Engage with mentors, coaches, and peers to gain new perspectives and enhance your leadership skills.

**6. Share and Inspire:**

- Share the insights and strategies you have learned with others in your network or organization.
- Inspire and mentor emerging leaders to help them develop their own leadership capabilities.

By implementing these steps and embracing the principles outlined in this book, you can drive meaningful change and achieve sustained success as a leader. Embrace the journey of continuous improvement and remain adaptable to navigate the dynamic landscape of leadership effectively.

**Appendices**

**Tools and Resources**

To support the implementation of future leadership concepts and strategies outlined in this book, consider the following tools and resources:

**1. Leadership Assessment Tools:**

- Myers-Briggs Type Indicator (MBTI): For understanding personality types and improving team dynamics. More Information
- 360-Degree Feedback Tools: To gain comprehensive feedback from peers, subordinates, and supervisors. Examples include SurveyMonkey and Culture Amp.

2. **Project Management Software:**

• Asana: For task management and team collaboration. Visit Asana

• Trello: For visual project tracking and management. Visit Trello

3. **Innovation and Creativity Tools:**

• MindMeister: For brainstorming and mind mapping ideas. Visit MindMeister

• IdeaScale: For crowdsourcing and managing innovative ideas. Visit IdeaScale

4. **Change Management Resources:**

• Prosci ADKAR Model: For structured change management. Learn More

• Kotter's 8-Step Change Model: For understanding the change process. Read More

5. **Leadership Development Programs:**

• Harvard Business School Online: Offers various leadership and management courses. Explore Courses

• Coursera: Provides online courses from leading universities on leadership and management. Visit Coursera

6. **Books and Publications:**

• "Leaders Eat Last" by Simon Sinek: A book on leadership and team dynamics.

• "The Innovator's Dilemma" by Clayton Christensen: A classic on innovation and disruption.

7. **Networking and Professional Associations:**

• LinkedIn Groups: Join professional groups related to leadership and management.

• American Management Association (AMA): Provides resources and training for leaders. Visit AMA

**Checklist**

Here's a quick reference checklist to help you implement the key strategies from this book:

1. **Vision and Strategy:**
   - Define a clear and inspiring vision for the future.
   - Develop strategic goals aligned with the vision.

2. **Innovation:**
   - Create an environment that encourages and supports innovation.
   - Implement processes to evaluate and execute new ideas.

3. **Digital Transformation:**
   - Integrate digital tools and technologies into your leadership strategy.
   - Address and overcome digital transformation challenges.

4. **Change Management:**
   - Develop a comprehensive plan for managing change.
   - Allocate resources effectively for successful implementation.

5. **Team Building:**
   - Build and manage a high-performing, diverse team.
   - Foster a collaborative and inclusive team environment.

6. **Ethical Leadership:**
   - Uphold ethical standards and build trust within the organization.
   - Integrate social responsibility into leadership practices.

7. **Communication:**
   - Enhance communication skills with all stakeholders.
   - Address misinformation and maintain transparency during crises.

8. **Cultural Change:**
   - Manage and develop organizational culture to support change.
   - Measure and analyze the impact of cultural changes.

9. **Crisis Management:**
   - Prepare and implement strategies for effective crisis management.
   - Maintain clear communication with your team during crises.

10. **Performance Measurement:**
    - Establish and track key performance indicators.
    - Analyze results and make necessary adjustments.

11. **Generational Innovation:**
    - Leverage generational diversity to drive innovation.
    - Manage and motivate multi-generational teams effectively.

12. **Personal Growth:**
    - Set and pursue personal development goals.
    - Seek feedback and engage in continuous learning.

13. **Strategic Analysis:**
    - Conduct thorough strategic analysis of internal and external factors.
    - Develop and implement effective strategies based on analysis.

14. **Sustainability:**
    - Integrate sustainability principles into leadership practices.
    - Implement and track sustainable initiatives.

15. **Cross-Cultural Collaboration:**
    - Foster effective collaboration across different cultures.
    - Manage and leverage cultural differences for enhanced teamwork.

16. **Case Study Analysis:**
    - Study successful case studies and extract key lessons.
    - Apply insights from case studies to your leadership practices.

By utilizing these tools and following the checklist, you can effectively implement the strategies discussed in this book and drive successful leadership and organizational outcomes.

# References

Here is a comprehensive list of sources and references used in this book, including complete URLs for each resource:

1. **Books and Articles:**

- Kotter, J. P. (1996). Leading Change. Harvard Business Review Press.

Amazon Link

- Sinek, S. (2014). Leaders Eat Last: Why Some Teams Pull Together and Others Don't. Portfolio Hardcover.

Amazon Link

- Christensen, C. M. (1997). The Innovator's Dilemma: When New Technologies Cause Great Firms to Fail. Harvard Business Review Press.

Amazon Link

- Drucker, P. F. (2006). The Effective Executive: The Definitive Guide to Getting the Right Things Done. HarperBusiness.

Amazon Link

2. **Leadership Assessment Tools:**

- Myers-Briggs Type Indicator (MBTI):

Myers-Briggs Official Website

- 360-Degree Feedback Tools:

SurveyMonkey: SurveyMonkey Website

Culture Amp: Culture Amp Website

3. **Project Management Software:**

- Asana:

Asana Website

- Trello:

Trello Website

4. **Innovation and Creativity Tools:**

- MindMeister:

MindMeister Website

- IdeaScale:

IdeaScale Website

5. **Change Management Resources:**

- Prosci ADKAR Model:

Prosci ADKAR Website

- Kotter's 8-Step Change Model:

Kotter Inc. Website

6. **Leadership Development Programs:**

- Harvard Business School Online:

Harvard Business School Online Website

- Coursera:

Coursera Website

7. **Networking and Professional Associations:**

- LinkedIn Groups:

LinkedIn Groups Website

- American Management Association (AMA):

American Management Association Website

About the Author

YOUSIF BSHIR is an acclaimed leadership expert and visionary strategist known for his groundbreaking work in future-oriented leadership. With extensive experience in guiding organizations through transformative change, YOUSIF brings a wealth of knowledge in strategic planning, innovation, and ethical leadership. His insights and methodologies are designed to help leaders navigate the complexities of the modern world and achieve sustainable success.

YOUSIF's career spans various industries, and he has been recognized for his ability to drive positive organizational change and foster a culture of continuous improvement. He is a sought-after speaker and consultant, dedicated to empowering leaders to excel in a rapidly evolving global landscape.

For more information about YOUSIF BSHIR and his work, please visit

Contact Information

Email: Yousif.Bshir5@gmail.com

LinkedIn: https://www.linkedin.com/in/yousifb?utm_source=share&utm_campaign=share_via&utm_content=profile&utm_medium=ios_app

Instagram: https://www.instagram.com/yousif_bshir?igsh=MXZpczlzOHpwZ2g0&utm_source=qr

Phone: +971 506606715

www.ingramcontent.com/pod-product-compliance
Lightning Source LLC
Chambersburg PA
CBHW062121220526
45471CB00010B/3824